# Naked
# Wild and Free
# in the
# Grand Canyon

## Rowing and Roaming

## Cameron Powers

Naked Wild and Free in the Grand Canyon
Rowing and Roaming
First Edition

Original Copyright © 2015 by Cameron Powers
Published by GL Design, Boulder, Colorado, USA

All rights reserved. No part of this book may be reproduced in any form or by any electronic or mechanical means including information storage and retrieval systems without permission in writing from the publisher, except by a reviewer, who may quote brief passages in a review.

Library of Congress Control Number: 2016902309
ISBN: 1-933983-20-5
ISBN Complete: 978-1-933983-20-2

Thanks to my friendships with some wonderful folks in Steamboat Springs, Colorado, I was able to row down the Colorado River and some of its upper tributaries for several long delightful exploratory river trips from 1969-1975.

I kept enough of a journal on one of those trips to provide a glimpse into our happy river pirate style.

Many more people were involved than I have mentioned here. The names I have used are fictitious and the character personalities are composites. I am deeply grateful to all those who were involved. We were living on some kind of natural edge and having more fun than we even realized at the time.

Author: Cameron Powers

# Contents

.

# I stood in reverie on the rim, watching

the giant orange ball descending inevitably to slip behind the ragged horizon over the canyon in the west. With the big orange guardian gone, a wind arose which nearly knocked me of my feet. What a night-bound rush of exuberant air came blasting out of the canyon's throat! All the night demons and spirits had been wide awake and waiting their chance to open their doors and rush into their favorite nocturnal places once the sun was gone. What a tumult they made! I found myself standing on the brink of the canyon with a giant musical bellow being squeezed out of my chest into the flurry of winds and spirits, my spine charging and recharging and discharging shrilly in every direction. It's all I could do to just stand there on my feet before the sudden force of that canyon-full of breath.

The birds loved it. They were hurling themselves over the rim of the canyon, swimming in the air the way we swim under water through a cataract: plummeting over my head and out into the fathomless space over the gorge like little banners flapping in the wind! There he goes, a tiny wren with wings blown back over his head tumbling past the jagged rock, making desperate flaps with those short little wings, just barely succeeding in avoiding being dashed against the naked rock. Every night, without even knowing why, he'd be there hurling himself again and again over the edge.

Two or three hours a day on the river was enough for us. We needed most of our time free for climbing and exploring. Today we had climbed up to the rim south of the river. We descended back to the boats with the very last light of sunset, the yucca plants still greeting us with their giant stalks hung with pendulous white flowers.

We reached the river on the canyon floor and all peeled off our clothes for that first plunge back into the refreshing waters.

Those who had remained near the boats offered us plates of endless stew... Beans and rice... We spread out plastic ponchos on the river beach and fell asleep for the night.

We arose and got on down the river... There was the usual mad confusion of ropes, loading and unloading, hugging, wrestling and kissing, more swimming, popping open cans of beer... We shoved off, ran Horn Creek and Salt Creek rapids, and set up camp for the night five miles downstream, at the top of Granite Rapids.

Quiet time... Sensuality and backrubs...

The big percussion waves in the rapids at the bottom of Hermit Creek were enough to bring us all into focus on the next day. Feet braced against the cross-beam on the bow, anchored to the end of the 14-foot oar, the living link between the boat and the river, I felt myself come more fully to life. Running the very center of the water's tongue, we plunged over the apex of wave

after wave, until we found ourselves in troughs which seemed capable of flipping our twenty-foot boat end-for-end. My old feeling for the bow, the cockpit of the boat, rushed into me, I was home once again, perched on a crest, peering eight feet

down into the trough below, willing and ready with the oar...
anxious, eager for the boat to take the plunge, do its worst! I
challenge you to spin this boat, turn her broadside! Nestled for

a moment in the bottom of a trough, oar deeply embedded in the heart of the oncoming wave, the bowman's job is to deliver just the right stroke and keep the craft's trajectory straight and true. He wrestles with the end of the oar the way the cattleman wrestles a steer to the ground. He wrestles to stay on the boat. The river wrestles to throw, drag or catapult him off. Pearce and Ludwig, twin companions on the stern endure the identical fight, each likewise locked with the river through fourteen feet of oar. Old Silas, beard wagging, entwining arms and legs through the rigging, locks himself to the mast and peers down-river through his binoculars... I felt whole once again, freed, rid of my civilized and not-so-civilized obsessions. The river and the canyon, gleaming its rocky glory at me from all four sides, crushed those vague and uncertain dreams and left me standing, clean and reborn, bolt upright on the bow. Pearce and Ludwig grinned at me rapturously from their oars on the stern, likewise whole and victorious, chests hairy and splendid in the sun, eager for more.

River! By what right do you make these decisions? Building me up and breaking me down, always saving me in the end! I must admit, life is recklessly sweet. And the river always brings me back! I can hurl myself naked into the worst of her waters, and she always coughs me back unharmed to her shores.

Three miles below Hermit Creek we pulled off to survey Crystal rapids from the shore. There is a pulsing mound of frothing water and a hole below it in the lower part of Crystal which is not the place to go. All fourteen of us, both boatloads, stood goggle-eyed on the shore and watched it seethe. I was aware of Sonia, Sandra and Joy, the three women on our boat. Just before we cast off to run Crystal, Joy came and nestled her chin into the crook of my arm and gave me a deep and terror-stricken gaze. I gave her a re-assuring squeeze on the shoulder and down we went, passing within a few feet of the incredible haystack water mound which towered above us on the left and which then subsided into a chasm, swirling and sucking, into which we cold peer with awe, as we passed safely along its edge. Once again jubilant, Ludwig and Pearce and I grinned fiercely at each other, old Silas's beard wagging as he guffawed in our midst. Not far behind us, Abner brought his craft safely through the chute, arms waving, faces triumphant, Murdock and Scott hanging their arms loosely over the twin oars on the stern, cheering loudly at us, fresh from the fray. Joy's face is ecstatic, eyes burning out into the hot canyon sunshine, electricity in the depths of her brain.

Thinking to moor briefly on the shore for lunch, we nestle into a crevice in the black canyon wall on our left, just above Tuna Creek. But no sooner, alas, has Ludwig leapt nimbly onto a tiny flat space at the bottom of the granite wall, stern-line in hand, than the swirling current has somehow plucked the boat, all twelve hundred pounds of her, back into her grasp. In a moment we have rounded the corner, Ludwig has let go his futile tug on the stern-line, and he is out of sight behind the wall of the gorge, which plunges vertically into the edge of the churning river. Rowing frantically, we succeed in hugging the wall

and pull into the next eddy on our left. Below us is the roaring of yet another of the string of rapids which adorn the bottom of this part of the canyon. We could see that Ludwig would have a good chance of reaching us by simply committing himself to the river, swimming to hug the wall as we had done with the boat, but how was he to know that? He was trapped behind a vertical wall which obstructed all view of what lay below, con-

fronted only by the roar of unseen tumult somewhere around the corner. We waited, life ropes in hand, waiting to see the bobbing orange form of a man in a life jacket committed to the river. None came. Looking above us we shook our heads uneasily. The black granite wall ascended sheer and high above us, but gradually we came to accept that it must be along systems of tiny little ledges that Ludwig would be seeking to reach us. Pearce and Silas and I simultaneously took to the rock.

"Here's a way!" we would shout from our separate exploratory courses when we surmounted still higher ledge systems on the wall. Gradually, each of us fanning out along each ledge until the next passage upwards was found, worked our way to a ledge system 300 feet above the river along which we could travel back upstream. God only knows what it was like for Ludwig on the other side, but after 45 minutes of this, with old Silas finally out in the lead, we heard an answering shout from around the corner of a great buttress. One small ledge on the buttress, the crux of our reunion, proved traversable.

"I did the best I could," Ludwig grinned at us, in his crazy German accent, hands and legs full of cactus spines, to which he was apparently oblivious. "I didn't know what had happened to you guys, so I thought I might find you up here on this cliff!" he guffawed.

Abner's boat had tied up to wait in another cleft below, but on the other side of the river. With obvious relief they watched us come floating and grinning down past them, Ludwig firmly aboard again. There had not been a damn thing they could do to get to us or help us. The seven souls on each boat looked at each other with fresh concern, realizing that they must hold their lives together by themselves, separate and independent crews.

Soon after we unloaded our boats that first night at Bass Creek, Abner signaled me to come over onto his boat. He had brewed peyote tea. By the time the moon rose, approaching fullness, over the rim of the inner gorge, I had tired of the conversation, and was yearning for a more primeval communion with the canyon. Grasping my old friend, the guitar, by the

neck, I climbed to the summit of a nearby rock spur and began to sing into the moon-bathed shadows of the canyon, yearning for the company of the spirits which I hoped to call forth.

Uncertain of my effect on my comrades below, but played out, I began my descent from the spur after an hour or so. Joy was waiting for me on the rocks below.

"That was beautiful," she told me. Pleased that at least someone had enjoyed the mood, I sat down beside her. Little Joy. So thin, tiny. A wisp of a girl.

"I was terrified in Crystal today," she confided. "I've been terrified ever since I was swept overboard with Scott three years ago in Lava Falls. Coming down here again was a big move for me," she said. "I had this awful feeling that I'd never come back up out of those waters. Today on the boat, when we began our descent through Crystal, it suddenly occurred to me to throw my energy onto the canyon below the rapids, and you know, as soon as I felt it fastened, anchored down there, I knew we would make it. By the time we passed the hole I was no longer afraid. It's such a relief to somehow find your way through something you've been so afraid of for so long!"

Tiny little Joy! Such a brave little soul: Delicate as a bird! Long into the night we sat beside each other; then lay together naked on the sand beside the river. She kissed me, gently. Our bodies touched, her legs rubbing across mine… Allowing the feelings to arise from within us we entered another magic land…

The next morning Pearce and I set off up over the dry and stony plateau which stood between us and Bass Creek. Content to wander slowly, we inspected the plight of the cacti along the way.

"My God!" Pearce exclaimed. "I don't see how these poor guys manage to survive here. You have to hand it to 'em. They have to be tough. My God Look at that!" he says pointing

to a leathery plant just bristling with spines growing out of a crack high above the ground with roots in nothing but sun-baked, blazing, naked rock.

"I have to take pity on a fellow like him! He actually reminds me of myself, ugly fucker that I am!" he says, reeling with uproarious laughter, opening one of our canteens and pouring its contents onto the parched plant. "For sure you need this worse than I do!" he tells the plant, chuckling outrageously.

I gazed in amazement as my giant, hairy, two-hundred-twenty pound friend, bearded and barbarous, lavished affection on one he took to be of fellow kind: that withered cactus, clinging wretchedly to his waterless crack. I had to admit I could see the resemblance.

Descending to Bass Creek, we found Slevin and Nicole basking luxuriously naked in a cool pool, slick creek water bubbling over their shoulders. Pearce and I climbed into the water beside them, asking once more for stories from their recent journey to Istanbul...

Resuming our walk, naked except for our boots, up Bass Creek, we soon came upon the remains of one of Bass's camps. William Bass, stricken shortly before the turn of the twentieth century with heart problems, fled into the dry fastness of the Grand Canyon. Choosing this very creek, he set up a home down here which lasted him for the next forty years! Here, laid out in the bottom of the side canyon, were the remains of his frying pans, lanterns, shovels, picks, cans and bottles, a little testament to a man who mounted an absurd remedy onto an absurd predicament and wound up with something which didn't seem so absurd at all: a life in the bottom of the Grand Canyon!

Moving on up the creek another mile or two, we came out onto a wide flat rock shelf at the bottom of a beautiful little cascade. Monica and Murdock, our ship's Doctor, Sandra and Scott were already there. We spread ourselves out like so many lizards on the warm shelf of rock, ate what little goodies we had brought with us, and surrendered ourselves to what the canyon seemed to have in mind for us: sleep. Gradually bestirring ourselves one by one an hour or so later, we dipped casually into the stream, rubbed mud over each other's bodies and lay

down once more, more lizardine than ever, on our shelf in the sun, letting the mud dry, wrinkling, scaling and crusting deeply into the folds of our skin. Hearing footsteps ascending the

canyon from below, we crouched behind the rocks, dusky grey reptilian forms, and uttered menacing grunts. Abner and Joy were sprung upon, seized and carried off to the mud wallow to be smeared and be-reptiled as were the rest of us. The canyon seemed immobile, calm.

Later that night we began to sing a few tunes, quietly at first. I began singing to the moon and felt the satisfaction of harmony and romance arise. What an addict of the orgiastic musical frenzy I have become! Pearce's lone deep bass voice began climbing up under my songs from below. Monica added a slow and perfect rhythm on a tambourine. What a pleasure to be surrounded by the dancing bare breasted women! When Sandra and Joy began to dance naked beneath the moon, I remember feeling the connection and feelings moving out toward all the women in the world! We all fell asleep in the same spot and didn't move until morning.

Scott awoke early the next morning and went down below the waterfall where Bass Creek approached the river and climbed barefoot up a steep rock chimney. When Sandra and Monica returned from a nearby waterfall with the news that Scott was stuck and needed to be rescued, I confidently slung a rope over my shoulder and set out with Silas. We spotted

him grinning like a little bear from an improbably inaccessible crow's nest high above us. Silas put a couple of cans of beer in my pack and guffawed and chuckled away, beard jiggling and wagging as always.

"Lost your nerve?", he called up to Scott. "I'm sending Cameron up with a couple of cans of cold nerve!" The little bear grinned down at us and I began following his route up the crack, belayed by Silas. Not only steep and exposed, but crumbly and loose rock!

"Whatever possessed you to come up here?" I wanted to know.

"I thought it led out onto that big ledge above us," he explained. I wondered how he could possibly have thought that, but there he was perched in his tiny rocky notch, stranded. I managed to sling the rope over a pinnacle and give myself some protection. I had shoes on; Scott's bare feet swung in the air above me.

"I need a can of that cold nerve!" he chuckled. Before long we managed to rappel safely to the ground, amidst the continual stream of Silas' high-rolling humor. Silas abandoned his career as a miner a few years ago when the man standing next to him was crushed to death by an ore car. And he's been wandering around aimlessly above ground ever since with nothing but an uproarious sense of humor to sustain him... and a thirst for exploration which led us time and again into steep and tricky places.

Six years earlier, somewhere in the slick sculpted white rim sandstones above the Green River in Canyonlands, we had managed to rappel to safety from another high lip of stone. About six of us had set off to climb up and over from one side

canyon to another. But the descent was a mystery. We had no idea of what lay ahead. ...or rather, below... Choosing a cleft in the top of the cliffs we began a descent which took us hundreds of feet down through the secret canyon wall waterways. Time and time again we leapt off rock lips into pools of water below. It became obvious that even with our best rock climbing skills,

which were considerable in that crowd, we were committed. We would not be able to climb back up those slick sculpted walls. Finally we peered over the last lip in the system of eroded cracks. The floor of the canyon was visible below. But how far down was it? We were perched in an overhanging notch.

The descent was not possible to down-climb. It was beyond the vertical in a canyon wall with no hand or foot holds. Treading water in a pool we finally found a crack into which to drive an anchor for our ropes. But how far down was it? We had enough rope with us to descend 150 feet. Peering over the lip it looked like the vertical distance might easily be much more than that... What to do? Rappel down 150 feet and let go and fall the remaining distance? To our amazed relief the ropes almost reached the bottom and we lowered ourselves one-at-a-time like spiders and had only to let go and free-fall the last five feet or so.

By afternoon, we managed to get it together to shove off, wave goodbye to Scott's crow's nest, which we could see from the river, and float on down a few miles. Below us the black granite walls of the inner gorge appeared to rise higher, steeper, and the canyon began to twist more severely, making it nearly impossible to anticipate the exact locations of the rapids which lay ahead or to even find a place along the wall to stop and tie up. We eventually found a shelf to sleep on opposite Garnet canyon. It seemed the canyon had begun to weigh on our souls and the whole mood crumbled like a house of cards. We fell into deep and early sleep.

The next morning we woke up with Elves' Chasm just around the corner. A few minutes on the river and we were at its entrance, right at the point of a sharp bend in the canyon. Eager to find what lay above, we began scrambling up past waterfall after waterfall. Nature had not rendered the ascent impossible the way she so often does in those box canyons and we found our way up over shoulder after shoulder of rock. Our crews spread out, some staying to bask in pools below waterfalls by whose spirit they had been captured, while others climbed on up to the next. Pearce and I climbed together up to a high pool.

"How come these canyon walls look so familiar?" I was musing. "You don't suppose I have an ancestor who spent years living in canyons like these?"

"What I'm trying to figure out is whether I'm headed north or south," he replied.

"North or south?"

"Haven't you noticed how confused us green-eyed people always are?" he asked. "It's because we've got some ancestors in us from the north with blue eyes, and some from the south with brown eyes, and they're battling away inside of us trying to decide which way to head, back north or back south!" We looked at each other and realized we both had almost exactly the same mixture of brown and blue in our eyes!

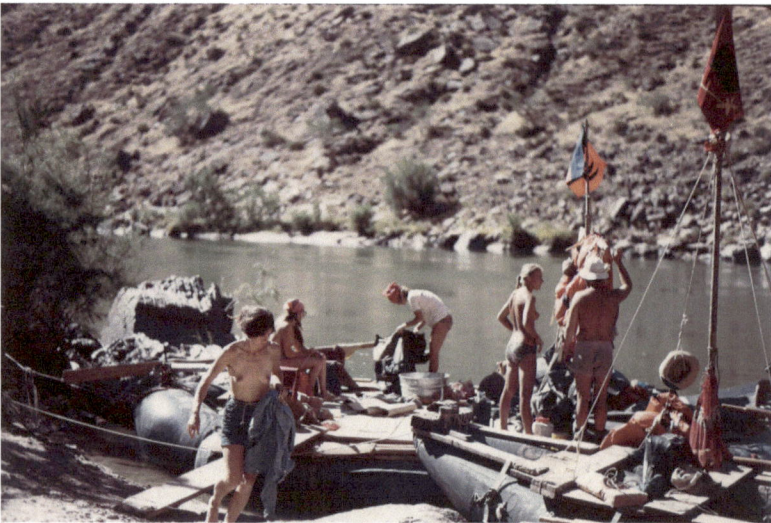

"That's why we never have single-minded opinions," he went on. "A man of pure blue-eyed stock sees things from one point of view and that's it. He doesn't have the opposite point of view tugging away inside of him. And it's the same with the brown-eyed folk. They've got one point of view: their brown-eyed point of view. Hell, I sure noticed that in my three years of wandering through Africa! Not a trace of my blue-eyed half could be found around anywhere to commiserate with! There were solid brown eyes from one end of the continent to the other. Shit, they can't even imagine the schizophrenia of the green-eyed man! But which way am I goin'? That's what I'm tryin' to figure out. I think it's south."

"Me too," I said. "The older I get, the dimmer those visions of the north woods get and the more familiar things feel south of the border..."

"When I was in Africa though," Pearce reminisced on, "I always wondered what that cloudiness the people sometimes have in their eyes meant. Some of the old men's eyes are so thick and black and cloudy that you wonder what it would be like to see the world through eyes like that!... I once knew an old man in Kansas whose eyes went bad. He just crawled out into his cornfield and lay down and died... eyes closed. I'd rather die with my eyes open..."

"You would? I'd always imagined dying with my eyes closed."

We both thought about that for a while. The huge eternally dripping wall above us played its watery music in the background, muffling itself with banks of mosses and lichens.

"I like to watch those movies that we all have going on in our heads, you know? I think if I were dying I'd want to be watching those..."

"Not me. I used to see those movies all the time when I was a child, but I kept seeing the same ones over and over, I got bored with them. I like it outside better. No, if I were dying I'd rather have my eyes open..." Pearce continued.

"That's probably why I got nearsighted in one eye," I figured. "'Cause I liked to watch those movies so much. With me they're never the same... never boring..."

Who should appear at this Point but Ludwig, the most blue-eyed man on the trip!

"We were just talkin' about livin' in the north versus livin' in the south," Pearce tells him.

"I don't think I could live in the south," Ludwig immediately volunteers. "People down there are pretty strange!"

"That's what we thought you'd think, judging by the color of your eyes!"

We both laughed. Then we proceeded to explain our green-eyed dilemma to him. He nodded his head. It seemed logical to him.

Slevin and Nicole came down from a still higher waterfall. The moment Nicole sat down among us I felt a change rip-

ple through the men. I felt the change in myself too. Suddenly the world gained another dimension again: the dimension of sweet and sour. I felt us all begin to strive toward the sweet. Nicole plops her juicy little body down amongst us and off we go. Everything's changed. The thoughts no longer float in of their own accord. They are plucked out of internal sacks, planned and directed... Each man begins striving. Only Slevin watches with detachment, unaware of the transformation. After all, he spends all his time with her and no longer spends all his time flirting with her.

Back down at the lowest waterfall once again Pearce treated us all to a little dance on top of a rock high above the pool below, striking one pose after another.

Sonia and Silas, the two old leathery ones, joined us from wherever they'd been off together chewing nails, toughening their hides a bit more I suppose... Pearce finished his acrobatics with a magnificent plunge into the pool below.

"Thanks, Pearce," Sonia tells him. "I truly enjoyed that!"

'As the days pass in this canyon, life grows thicker. The very air seems to thicken... A person begins to walk with a sense of connection to the rocks, the water, the air, the sizzling sunshine, the heavy darkness of moonless times of the night... Then the connection to sense, spirit, the plants and animals thickens too... And there is a feeling of being drawn into the

swelling desire for contact with even greater depths of the canyon.

Joy and I were drawn that night into Blacktail Canyon, a narrow winding corridor, night air thick with the smell of damp rock. Besieged by the magnetism of this little canyon, we crept our way along its floor, pushing our slight tingling sense of fear ahead of us, surrounded by the amplified echoes of our own breathing. The sun finished setting and it there was no light left in that canyon. We had not brought lights. Deeper and deeper into the black labyrinth we slipped, until rounding a last corner we could make out the heavy darkness of a solid wall at the canyon's end, a waterfall... or at least it would be a waterfall were there enough water. A spine-tingling noise greeted us at the very moment we rounded that last corner and glimpsed the wall. Was it an owl? Perhaps he had glided ahead of us on silent wings, seeking to escape our advance. Or perhaps he liked his close little place at the very end of the canyon. In any case, he began to scold us now, hooting and howling at us, a vulnerable and pleading cry in his voice. The tones made the message unmistakably clear.

"Don't! Don't! Don't come any closer!" he pleaded. "You're terrifying me whoever you are! This is my canyon; won't you please stay out of it! You're squashing me to the last limit! Please don't drive me out of my very own place!!!" We immediately retreated, amazed by what we had heard. It was with a gentle sense of relief that we eventually emerged out into the comparative openness of the greater canyon. We nearly stumbled over Sonia and Silas who were asleep in the entrance, no doubt lured by the same magnetism.

The next day we returned and found ways to ascend the waterfalls in the bottom of the same canyon until it opened out into a broad red canyon above, dry and hot enough to bake your brain except for one magic place where a few drops of water squeeze out of a crack in the wall. Beneath the water lay a rattlesnake, placidly coiled. He was a big one, with about

two inches of rattles on his tail. Nearly the whole bunch of us congregated up there: Abner, Silas, Sonia, Murdock, Slevin and Nicole, Joy, Sandra, Pearce and myself. The snake didn't seem to mind. The whole crowd of us stood around him and he made not a move of his body nor a shake of his rattle until Pearce, seized by some desire to see something happen, gave

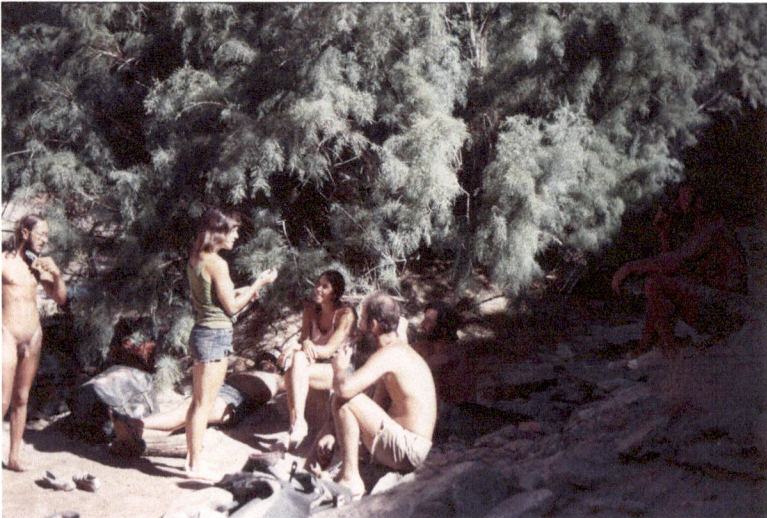

a low growl at the snake. The snake knew what kind of sound that was! No doubt about it! Instantly commencing to buzz, his coiled body visibly tensed. Pearce growled again and the snake slipped rapidly into the high weeds growing in the moist ground below the water hole.

"Hey! What 'd you do that for?" Slevin exclaimed. "I liked him better out here where I could still see him!"

Giving the weeds a wide berth we ascended a ways further on up the scorching canyon. That dry canyon soon began to look monotonous to us. Around every corner lay more fried, broken, red rock. Discouraged, hot and thirsty, Pearce and I found a rock shelf in the shade and made ourselves comfortable on it for a while. I found a little scorpion sitting quietly on a ledge. Pearce gazed at the little fellow for a while, and then

began tickling the end of its sting-
er with his finger. The scorpion did
not seem to mind; did not move;
made no attempt to either sting
or escape. All the while, Pearce
looked like he knew exactly what
he was doing. The huge man just
did not seem able to bring himself
to fear little insects...

Back at the mouth of the little canyon by the river we
cooked a leisurely and delicious dinner. The usual: tortillas,
beans, onions, cabbage, potatoes, plenty of beer... coffee... Abner brought out his bottle of 150-proof rum! Tonight is the
night of the full moon. With wide open eyes we watched the
brilliant phosphorescence of its light descend the west wall of
the canyon, making the rock as clearly luminous as it is by day
- perhaps even more so, for the eye is drawn to drink of that
magnificent white light.

Slevin and I pulled out our battered old river guitars;
Scott sent vibrant banjo notes full into the echoing canyon;
Pearce hunched over the washtub bass, like a huge gopher
stroking his own fur, deep booming notes pounding out over
the river. All night long we played. The ladies sang, laughed,
danced, beat out rhythms on the planks of the boat upon which
we all sat. Sandra, cute and smiling; Monica, stately and holy,
a firm body with firm breasts, a firm sense of rhythm; Joy, fluttering, a little bird; Nicole, brown and womanly, a nymph of
the waters! Hour after hour passed... unnoticed by us. The
moon drew our energy out like a huge syphon.

Effortlessly, ecstatically, our bodies played and danced.
Scott, safely down from his stranded perch in the rocks, thank
god, body as tight and heavy as the little bear, began playing

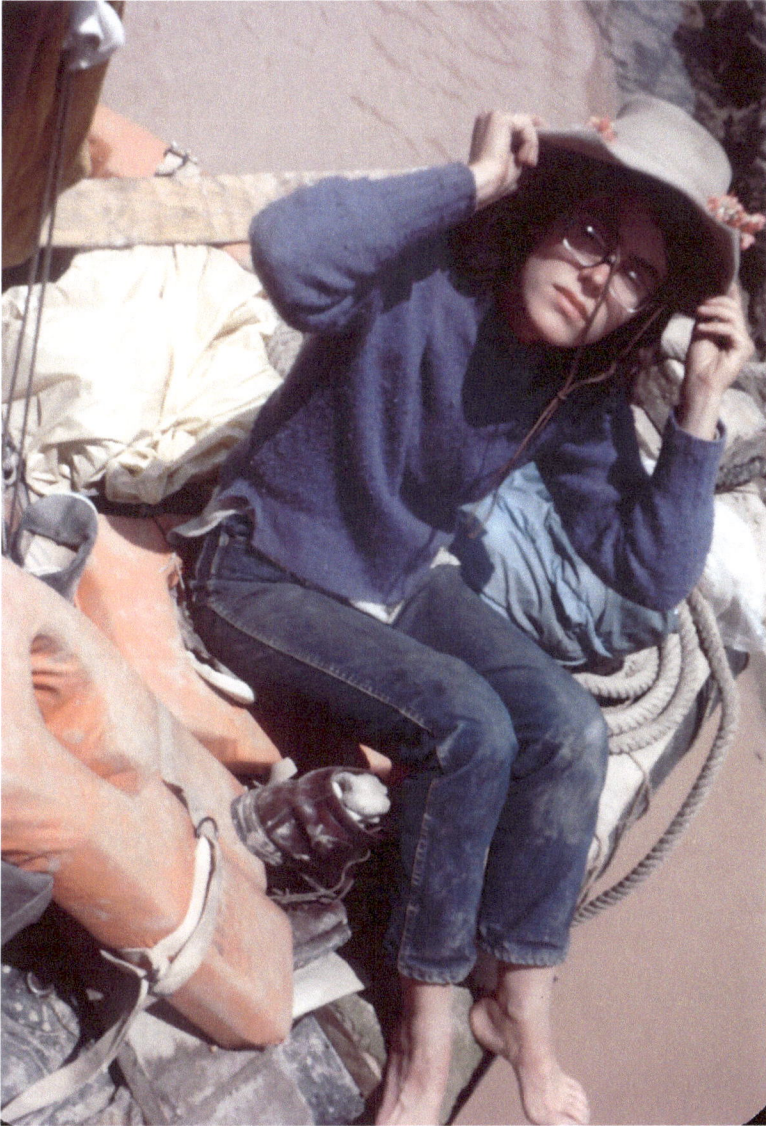

that banjo with a fury! And never before had I heard the deep booming notes emerge from a washtub bass so exactly in tune, on pitch and precise: Pearce had entered a washtub trance and remained in its clutches throughout the night. The moon swung clean across the breach of sky open to us through the canyon above. It seemed  too bright to behold with a direct gaze! And just as it finally neared the rim and was on the brink of vanishing, a final musical orgasm shook our bodies and we all dove into the swirling river simultaneously!

The next day I gave Pearce the bow oar, the captain's responsibility, through Bedrock and Dubendorfer rapids. Perched on the bow like a giant gorilla, the man was capable of wrenching the boat sideways against the current with incredible surges of strength.

Day by day we were regaining our animal selves. I felt that I would never again succumb to the civilized luxury of forgetting my healthy animal nature. No I would never let it peel off, fall away, evaporate, vanish into sleepy vestigial nothingness. I could not imagine myself ever again zombie-walking down a city street as if gliding through the atmosphere-less terrain of the moon, shorn of all connection with men and trees

who live and breathe in their own majesty. No, I would never again be capable of slumping limply into an armchair, mind and senses dull and vacant...

Trying for the first time to read the waters, judge and steer down the river, Pearce looked ridiculously nervous and ill-at-ease. I could barely suppress my grins as I stood behind him, ostensibly ready to coach if necessary... I knew that his in-

stincts would tell him which way to pull even if his mind would not... that his body had, the strength to correct even last minute errors. Down through the rapids we plunged, drawn by the raging and tumbling current toward the giant flat-topped slab which lies in the center of Bedrock waiting to trap a boat careless enough to come too close and find itself tossed like a shell onto a beach... Body wound tight as a winch, Pearce heaved us off and away from the sharp edge of the rock, desperate in the strain of his new responsibility. He loved it. Ludwig and Silas eyed him calmly from the stern. They too had known that he would manage magnificently.

Sonia cried, "Good going Pearce!" She was secretly in love with him, and she stood up from her perch beneath the mast, tawny little body straining with sinews, face aglow, cheering him on. Sandra's face wore the same trusting aura with softness, a gentle but spunky girl, content with her beauty, content with the canyon, the river...

Joy beamed like a little star, no longer submerged in fear and awe. She had left that behind above Crystal! Through Dubendorfer she cried "Yay! Yay!" with every stroke of Pearce's blade; every surge and plunge of the boat through the foam; every cleansing deluge of icy river water which swept over the bow and across the deck, engulfing us up to our necks in foam!

"Move right! Move left! Hard left!" came Pearce's commands from the bow as he peered down the river and threaded

our course through chutes and troughs, avoiding the humps and cones and fishtails of water which betray the presence of buried rock.

"Pop! Pop! Pop!" go the opening beer cans under Silas' deft supervision once we've passed the tumult. Gentle river ahead now. We gaze at the streak of blazing blue sky above us between the black and red canyon walls. Close behind us floats

the other boat, Abner waving cheerfully from the bow, Murdock and Scott staunchly on the stern...

Pearce and I volunteered to mastermind a nameless stew for dinner that night at the bottom of Tapeats Creek. Ludwig, visibly unhappy at the idea of having us two for cooks, began preparing a nice light pot of chicken tetrazzini, carefully measuring the ingredients with far northern blue-eyed meticulousness.

"Dat's all right," he said cheerfully. "You guys go ahead and make some nameless stew just however you like. I'll just make up some of this chicken here so that, you know, ve haf something else to eat!"

Pearce and I worked away on our brew. We put in a little of whatever seemed handy.

Slevin came by to watch, getting into the spirit of things. Before anybody could stop him, his arm reached out and casually deposited a full can of jalapeño peppers into Ludwig's tetrazzini! Divine inspiration!

Ludwig had been looking the other way. Without having noticed the addition, he took a big bite of his tetrazzini and we saw him immediately stomp off into the bushes to cool off, smoke pouring out of both ears while the rest of us chuckled around the campfire. Eventually he returned.

"I decided it is actually quite delicious!" he announced and put some more of the fiery tetrazzini in his cup.

Abner, Silas and Sonia had already set off to make camp a few miles up the creek below Thunder Falls, and the next day Pearce and I took off after them. We knew that their plan was to spend the day in Tapeats Cave, which lay a few miles up the canyon beyond Thunder Falls and Thunder Cave.

The canyon has a gushing, formidable creek plunging along its floor over waterfall after waterfall, and the route to Thunder Falls follows trails which zigzag up and down the parched talus slopes above. A little campground complete with metal outhouses astonishes visitors below Thunder Falls. But above, the route up Tapeats Creek is a terrible tangle. Anyone with the spirit of boyhood left in his feet will love it. Wade up the creek, climb a waterfall, work your way along a tiny ledge until it breaks loose and sends you plunging into the pool below. The margins of the cascade are anything but dry and barren. Cottonwood trees twist together with tamarisk and present impassable tangles. The walls above are too steep to offer rapid alternatives, unlike the exploited talus slopes below, but the determined creek climber easily finds ways through.

Two hours above the campground below Thunder Falls we climbed up into the final cul-de-sac, .a giant box canyon in the redwall. Few clamber up there and there is no clear trail. With time and luck we would have eventually found the entrance to the cave, but we were spared the effort. We heard the sound of voices.

Silas, Sonia and Abner had just emerged from an hour underground, carbide lamps still aflame on their helmets. Abner and Sonia had had enough, were standing shivering in the sunshine, delighted, to have emerged from those frigid underground passages. Silas wanted to go back in and go further. The miner in him hadn't expired after all. And we were just the new team he needed to make this greater penetration, so in we crept. The entrance to the cave is big enough to drive a car into, but it soon narrows and tightens until one has to stoop. This entrance is but a side passage, however, off the sumptuous underground river which spills out into the sunshine through

another cleft in the redwall and forms Tapeats Creek. We scurried along behind Silas, twisting this way and that through a
labyrinth of little passages which he already had deciphered.
Wondering if my memory could serve an unchaperoned exit, I
doubted it. But Silas would know. The thundering and crashing
of the great river grew louder and we emerged into the main

passage. Our lamp beams faded into the blackness but illuminated patches of ceiling high above us. We were inside a truly monstrous tunnel. I was chilled by the sight.

Anxious to speed to the limit of his previous exploration, Silas danced forward, upstream inside the giant tube. Eventually I realized that what I perceived as a thundering roar was just the amplified echoes of trickling waters. The floor of the river did not descend abruptly and the water flowed single-mindedly, but not chaotically. Back and forth we meandered, jumping from slippery rock to slippery rock.

We had surpassed Silas' previous turn-around point. An occasional behemoth splash announced the loss of someone's footing. We edged along the sides of the tunnel and then clambered over the heaping debris of mammoth roof collapses which choked the passage from time to time. Surmounting such mounds, we were brought near the roof and could caress occasional stalactite forests, tiny but perfect.

Chattering about mythological cave monsters, Silas led us over the mounds of caved-in roof. Settled over the rocks, as light and weightless as moon dust, was a fine layer of powdered silt. Our feet padded noiselessly through the stuff.

Disquietingly enough, we could make out the footprints of some lone man who had preceded us into the depths of this cave but who had left no trace of an exit. I stared at the tracks wondering how many years or decades or hours ago they might have been made, my chin in my hand, pupils bulging wide in the dark.

We peered through the blackness of the underground canyon ahead. Not a ledge, not a stone protruded from the clear cold water. The walls plunged sheer into the depths of the subterranean fluid.

"I bet there's a syphon up there!" Silas surmised, pulling off his britches. Lowering himself into the river until he was nothing but a head with a little carbide flame licking out of its forehead, he paddled off upstream and disappeared from sight. Pearce and I squatted on the rocks, peering after him.

From time to time we heard garbled exclamations, apparently made by Silas to himself as he made further discoveries and deciphered the secrets of the cavern. Eventually he reappeared, water glistening in his beard, wide row of teeth clenched against the cold.

"Yup, I think that's it," he announced. "The siphon! The roof comes down to meet the water up there. Of course it's always possible that one of those little side passages might lead around into another room further up, and I didn't squeeze all the way into every last one of them. I was starting to get a little cold," he concedes, eyes gleaming with fierce mischief, still enveloped in his world of goblins, pirates and elves... He's a little disappointed not to have had a brush with a dragon or serpent; not to have stumbled across a gleaming magic jewel or inadvertently poked his elbow into the soft underbelly of a bear! Still muttering to us and to himself about the numerous possibilities which might still lie undiscovered in those farthest reaches, he pulled himself back into his pants and we made ready to return to that now inconceivably distant realm of brilliant hot sun and sparkling canyon waters all shaded over with the waving green fronds of cottonwood trees...

As so often happens in the wilderness, the shape of the land funneled us along an unseen route, its signs and blazes far too subtle to be noted by the conscious mind, yet powerful enough to direct the footstep of man after man along the same identical path... For some reason our route out proved distinct from our route in... And to my relief I saw the mysterious footprints heading out...

We returned to sleep below Thunder Falls. I spread my poncho out on the ground and lit a candle beside it. A perfect little white scorpion marched out onto the middle of it. Although convinced that dozens of his friends must be jerkily waddling under the weight of their own immense stingers only inches away from me in the bushes, there was nothing for it but to lie down on the oven-hot ground and see what I could do about falling asleep for the night. Some animal a good deal larger than any scorpion had been scurrying noisily through the bushes around us for hours. And now it had the audacity to scramble hurriedly across the small of my back as I lay on my belly on my poncho, hot and scared of scorpions, waiting for some blessing of drowsiness.

Sitting up and quickly putting a match to my candle, I beheld a spotted skunk the size of a large kitten dapperly

scratching himself beside my feet. He seemed to have trust-ingly accepted me as camp-buddy for the night, apparently of-fering me nothing but camaraderie and friendship. My uneas-iness melted into his easy nonchalance and I felt glad to have such a cute little companion. Nor did my candle flame reveal any more encroaching scorpions.

The next day Pearce and I strolled across the baked expanse of Surprise Valley, descending rocky switchbacks into the shaded, watercress-laden upper reaches of Deer Creek in the midst of the sizzling afternoon. We had left Silas with Sonia and Ludwig, clambering up the ledges below Thunder Cave, bound for another day's exploration of the chilly black innards of the rock. They had agreed to bring the boats down without us and pick us up at the mouth of Deer Creek late in the day. Whiling away the afternoon hours, we slept deeply in the shade of those vast cottonwoods, rousing ourselves at last to descend to the river. Deer Creek plunges down a gorge so narrow and steep that its bottom is lost from sight below the undulations and bulgings of the constricting walls. Peering over the edge at its top we could only guess at its possible depth.

Following a trail along the west edge of the gorge, we soon emerged on the heights above the river. Then, having forsaken the trail, which seemed to veer off too far toward the west, we descended the ragged canyon wall, creeping as best we could through briar patches and hopping over little cracks and ledges until we reached the tamarisk swamp below. Beating our way upriver through the dense tangle, we eventually emerged at the mouth of Deer Creek.

We glanced up over the river and saw both boats go careening by, held fast into the center current, oarsmen struggling valiantly but without effect to make progress toward our shore. Giving up the fight, the boats made for the opposite side of the river and soon could be seen tied securely against the far shore a half mile downstream.

I remembered a similar situation six years earlier further up river. After a long hike up and over the ridge from one canyon to another we found no one at our agreed-upon rendezvous camp spot. Gambling that our boats must have missed the landing, the two of us had ridden driftwood logs after dark down the river for half an hour in order to catch up to our boats.

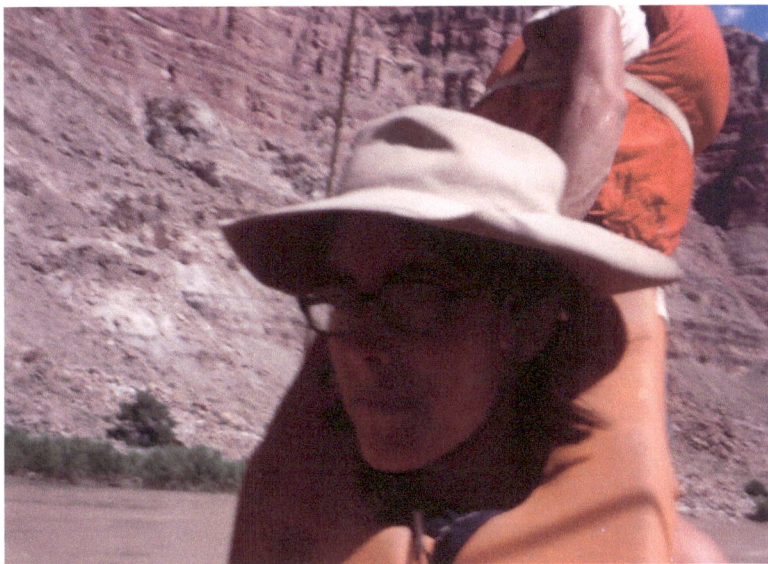

But now here we were, Pearce and I, thinking to find driftwood logs for the same reason. But our river-rat friends had seen us as they had passed. Before long the entire contingent of fellow naked pirates had marched up the rocks across the river from us and assembled, each gesticulating nonsensically at us. I couldn't hear a sound from any one of them above the rushing of the river, but I could suddenly see their chagrin at having stranded us on the other side vanish. With feverish delight, inspired we discovered later by Silas (who else?), they clumped together, every one of them, the bigger men getting down on their hands and knees side by side, backsides presented in our direction. Pearce and I gaped in astonishment as tier after tier went up until everybody had been incorporated. Joy perched precariously on the top of the naked human pyramid. We were being mooned by our friends. The famous insult we had devised for passing flotillas of motorized tourists was now being directed at me and Pearce. Exhausted, the pyramid tumbled into a flailing mass of naked flesh, from which individuals began to pick themselves up and reappear, urging us to plunge in and swim across.

Selecting a large grey snag of driftwood, we propelled ourselves out into the river behind it, our clothes in neat dry little piles on the floating log. The current did with us as it had done with the boats and deposited us on the thither shore. Pearce had never lost a heavyweight wrestling match in college, and he wasn't about to lose one now. Soon we had Silas captured, but transporting him to the river was another question since all 250 pounds of hay-bale buckin' Abner decided to intervene. We came to a standstill and Abner leaned back against a rock and lit up his corncob pipe… imperturbable, a quiet grin flickering around his chin while Silas chortled, beard a-shiverin' and a-waggin'…

''We saw you guys over there on the other side of the river, lost, unreachable, looking weak and forlorn, obviously

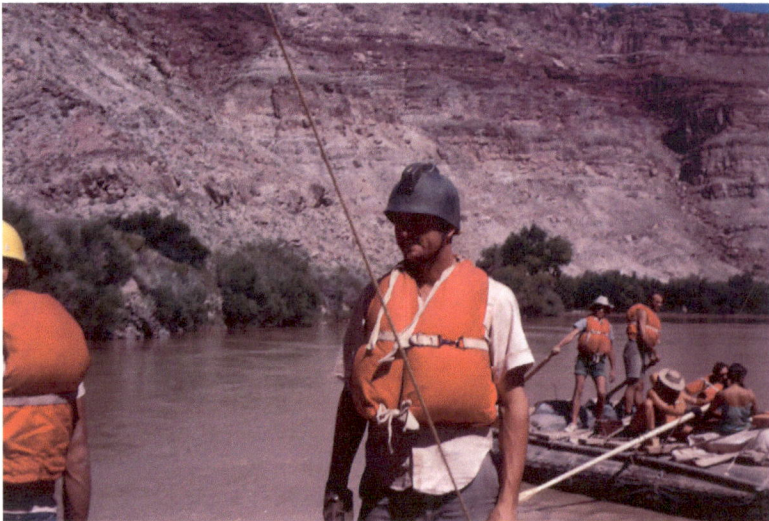

spent from your waterless ordeal in the desert, and I just knew, I just knew, that there was only one form of energy which could possibly save you and give you the strength to swim the river: 'Pyramid Power!' Now I know the scientific world still poo-poo's 'Pyramid Power', but..."

On and on he went, the endless carnival of Silas's self-spun world. Bellies jiggling with laughter, we all set about preparing dinner over the fire. Pearce plucked Sandra off her feet, slung her over his shoulder and disappeared into the night with her. The festive spirit was running high.

We put ashore next afternoon at the mouth of Kanab Creek, cursing the towns to the north which imbibe and excrete her water, transforming her into a vile, lifeless and stinking sewer. A short sojourn up the canyon was all I needed to drive me back down to the fresh air of the beach at its mouth.

Scott and Slevin twisted green tamarisk branches into rings and began a makeshift game of horseshoes. Before we knew it, that one little game had developed into a full-blown track meet, complete with races, wrestling matches, and handsprings into the river. Variations on the broad jump proliferated as fast as we could think them up: the standing broad jump, the running broad jump, the running jump followed by a headlong dive, a tuck and a somersault, leaving the jumper sitting on his ass, the marks made by his heels in front of him taken as the limit of his jump... Pearce outdistanced us all in every event, the incredible springs in his 220 pound body unleashing themselves in a frenzy of youth. Perfectly coordinated, his body arched through the air, tucking and flipping at the last possible moments with exact symmetry. All those years of football and wrestling... five hundred pushups a day... all that running and sweating under the hot Kansas sun... the heavy bar room brawls of later years... what else is a man intensively trained to struggle and fight to do with himself? Beneath the incredible sheath of muscle dwells a soul with the sensitivity of a psychic. Three years in Africa, most of it spent as the only white man in the witchcraft-laden labyrinth of Lagos, Nigeria sufficed to finally drain the man of enough of his surplus energy so that he can begin to pass for sane.

I felt myself hit from the side by another energy-charged bundle of solid muscle. Scott! My ears burning under the pressure of a headlock into which he deftly slipped me. Another bar room brawler of the mountain world, Scott had been flying through the air not so far behind the invincible Pearce, and now I felt myself like a gopher in the jaws of a bulldog, being shaken in his friendly grasp, listening to the gurgles of delight inside his chest. I lowered my head and embroiled myself like a twisting and writhing dragon in that pot belly of his. Eventually we headed to the boats for a beer.

Scott and I found ourselves bound together by thick bands of living, animal awareness. Our words tended to pop in the air like empty bubbles or dart for the rim like desperate sparrows. An extreme heaviness lay in the air as the daylight faded from the canyon. I looked above me at the black granite walls and judged that the inner gorge lay at its narrowest yet, right here. The south wall across from the mouth of Kanab Creek sways out over the river, shutting out the sky, shutting out the light... Back up on the beach a few of the women had decided to enter the races. Monica and Nicole flew across the sand, knees plunging, breasts wildly flopping, the last remnant of modern-day womanly decorum peeled off and let slip to the ground. The tension of all that incipient passion, the fruit of so much time spent under the weight of those black canyon walls, was bulging in our bellies. Scott and Slevin and I stood still by the boat exchanging long and slow words, words measured, tested and weighed... If our words crumbled on us we would be left with nothing but the incredible bands which wound through us like liquid steel. And that prospect was terrifying us tonight.

Desperately we stood like ivory statues, the night wind ruffling through our hair, grinding out word after word with utmost control and care. Not a single misunderstanding could be tolerated, nor could any inequality between us. At last anchored in unbreakable rapport, the three of us approached Pearce and Abner who were seated beneath the wall by the fire.

"Heavy shit!" Pearce pronounced sympathetically as we approached.

Abner's corncob protruded from beneath his hat, tobacco smoke curling up into the night. As he looked up at me I sensed the soul of an oriental behind those eyes... the Mongolian horseman... the smiling Buddha... rolling his eyes toward the black wall on the other side of the river he lightly acknowledged, "It's a heavy spot."

Scott had remembered that we still had one more refuge beyond words and soon strode back to the boat to reappear triumphantly bearing banjo and guitars. Pearce set up his washtub bass and notes sprang out into the night like meteor showers in the sky. Locked together by those same liquid steel bands, our arms and fingers began to strum as if attached to a single musician.

Scott and I caught glimpses in each other's eyes of such a fiendish identity that we recoiled at the sight: it was like looking into a mirror... The same creature was alive in both of us; he looked out both of our eyes, catching terrifying glimpses of himself whenever one pair of eyes looked into the other! And when it got right down to it, the music which that creature could play stripped souls like a raging brush fire leaving nothing but smoking black skeletons where flowered jungle had luxuriated only a moment before.

Terrified of the creature, and unwilling to surrender my body to the likes of him, I forcefully repossessed my soul and withdrew into a safer music... a safer song which I knew well and would not slip beyond my grasp... Scott also withdrew; drove the creature back out of himself, although he had been more willing than I to continue and follow its beckoning call...

"I see something in that wall!" cried a small female voice, excited, enraptured.., the voice of a little girl... Little Joy pointed at the tremendous looming south wall of the canyon. Our music hushed. "It's the face of a giant cat" she cried, lost in the depths of her vision. "A huge black shadow... It's like a gargoyle..."

Abner turned calmly toward her, removing the stem of the corncob pipe from between his teeth, and smiled knowingly. He had been looking long and deep at the same place. "To me it looks like a huge black cross," he said.

Relieved to wake up and find daylight suffusing the canyon once again the next morning, we climbed onto the river and rode it down to the mouth of Havasu Creek. Arriving in the heat of the noonday sun, we swam playfully in the pools at the confluence of the creek and the river. Diving off the boats, we swam up the side canyon, touching the rock walls with our fingertips from time to time, amazed at the sheerness of these gates... Yes, gates they were...

Another commercial boat crew approached and gave us a pile of their leftover groceries. We were happy to laugh and dance like the happy pirates they saw in us and sort through their gifts. They traveled so much faster through the canyon and didn't want to pack out their surplus foodstuffs. They were only a few hours away from the end of their run.

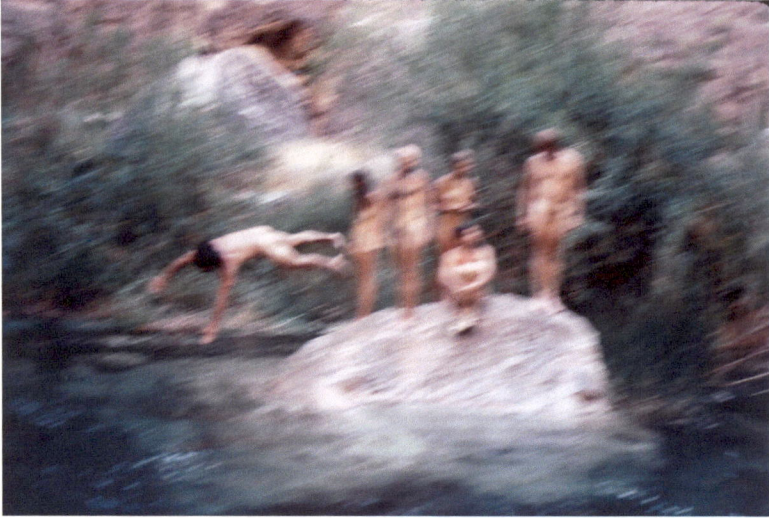

Swimming a few dozen yards further upstream we began to find breaks in those gates, and we clambered out onto the ledges, chutes and platforms of living rock. Perfectly suspended over the deep pools below, the invitation to dive was irresistible. Over and over again, for hours, we arched, jumped, tumbled and flopped into the water, from greater and greater heights, sometimes with six or eight of us linked arm in arm, entering the water simultaneously with huge bubbling blue splashes. A little higher up the creek we came across the first travertine pools: white, blue and purple mineralized bowls large and small, built intricately under the rushing milk-white waters of the creek year after year, millennium after millennium, like crystalline lace. We had entered the gates to the Garden of Eden. A lush green canopy of cottonwoods held the water's coolness snug against the canyon floor. Grape vines, planted years ago by the Havasupai Indians, strangled and choked together in overabundance, untended, ran wild and green over the beaches and rocks. High above, the orange and white redwall baked in the sun.

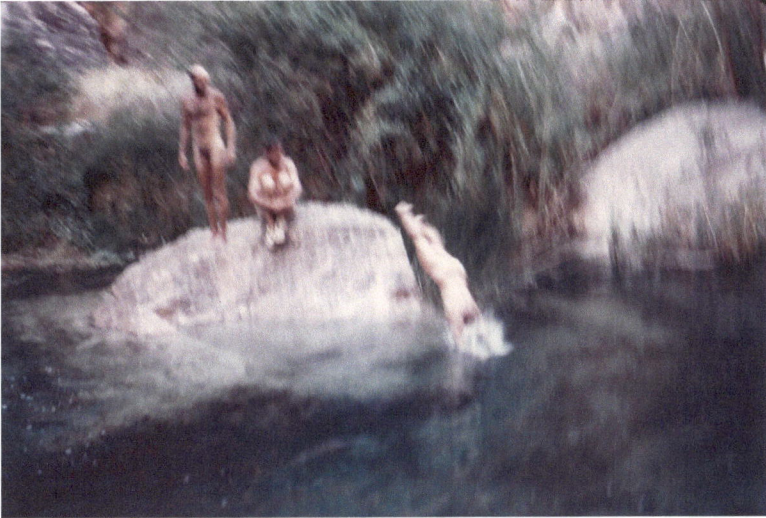

Securing the boats below, we filtered up into this newly discovered paradise, unmindful of each other, sprinkled out in groups of two or three. I set out with Abner and Pearce but outdistanced and lost them. Driven by a deep green longing in my belly to see more, enter more deeply into this cool and marvelous canyon, I kept plunging on ahead. With the last light of day, Slevin and Nicole suddenly appearing and became

my companions. I slithered and groped my way up the huge crystalline tears, draperies and splashes of the travertine tunnels beside Mooney falls. I had come close to ten miles up the canyon from the river. Here the Native Americans had chiseled a vertical labyrinth through the frills of mineralized rock. Possessed by the fascination of discovery, the three of us emerged on the precipices above, now separated by darkness from our companions below, and sought sleeping spots a bit further upstream on the packed earthen floor beneath the cottonwoods.

I remember nothing of the little conversation we indulged in around our little fire and dinner that night. I remember rolling up in my poncho in a hollow between two rocks, my body making a nest of the ground for the night... I remember worrying about Pearce and Abner... a vague sense of uneasiness... the possibility that one of them had somehow stumbled from a precipice in the dark... Why had they fallen behind and not caught up with us...?

Early in the morning I awoke. Slevin and Nicole still lay sound asleep, nestled in each other's arms. Taking care not to disturb them, I donned my shoes and crept back down the canyon. With the early morning silence still unbroken behind the cool, vine-shrouded canyon I remember relishing the chance to return to Mooney Falls, descend the travertine tunnels and

see exactly what that incredible tumbling fountain of water looked like. We had passed it by so hurriedly in the fading light the night before, desperate to find our way up the cliff side...

I worked my way back down the carved travertine staircases and found Abner and Pearce still camped and resting below the falls.

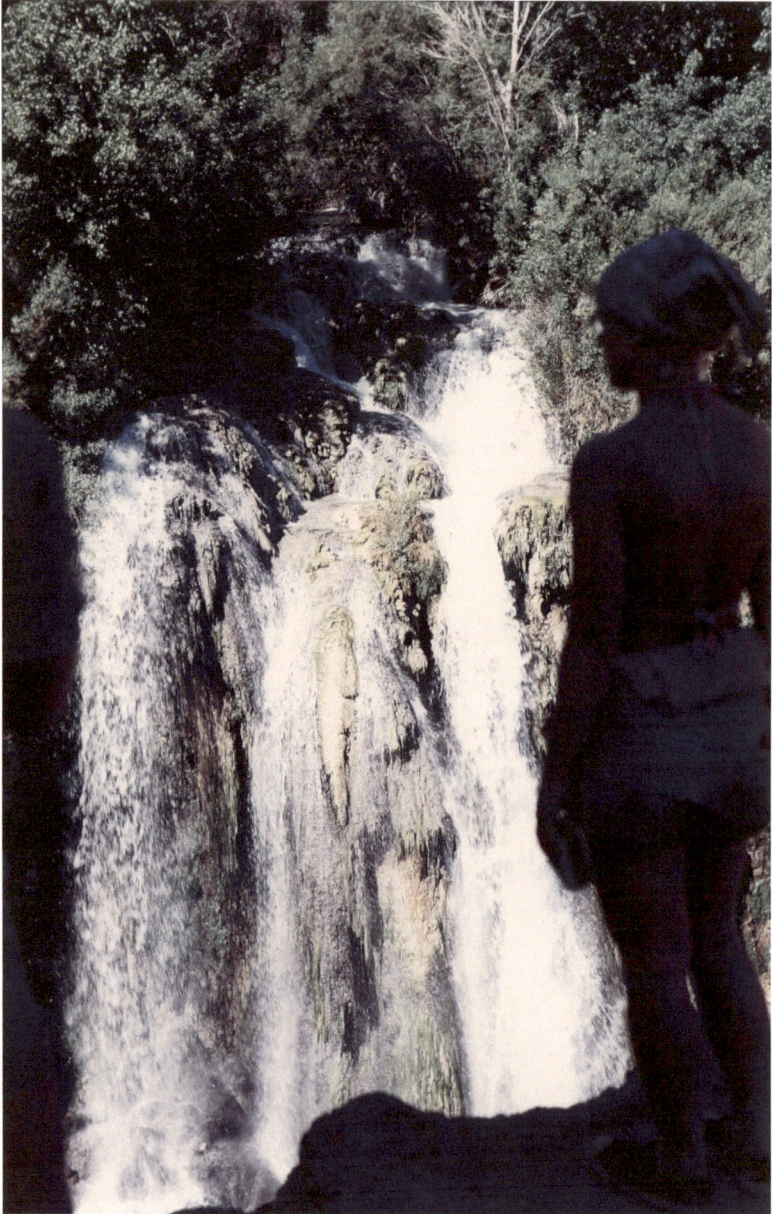

Soon we were joined by more or our crew and we swam
for a couple of hours below the falls before the prospect of more

explorations above lured us onward. Under the spell of Havasu Canyon we dissolved into timeless consciousness. We climbed to Havasu Falls and spent more hours swimming and diving.

"You know, there's a village right above us now," Silas shared…

Sure enough, after another hour's climb we were passing little mobile-home-like dwellings with TV antennas affixed to the roofs. In the center of the village we found a little restaurant. We entered with a feeling of strange amazement: it had been weeks since we had seen a cash register or thought about purchasing something with that green stuff called money. None of us, it seemed, was carrying any. We noticed the pie and hamburger for sale but had no means to pay for anything. We sat around a table thinking to perhaps hang out for a bit and drink a glass of water.

A couple of middle-aged Havasupai men entered the restaurant and informed us that we had needed to pay an entry fee of five dollars each in order to visit their village… Hmmm… We looked at each other and at them…

"Sorry… It seems that we didn't bring any money up from our boats on the river…" we explained.

"The fee is $5 apiece," they reiterated unsympathetically… no smiles… nothing.

We began standing up to leave and again commenting that we were sorry, made our way out of the little rustic restaurant.

"We don't welcome White Trash!" the Havasupai men snarled at us.

We scurried back through the village down toward the canyon.

It took most of the next day to descend the ten miles back to the river.

Abner placed his lips to the sawed-off hole in the end of the giant sea conch which dangles from the mast on his boat. His great chest inflating like a mammoth bellows, he sent a trumpet note echoing far up into Havasu canyon.

All having arrived back to the river, we went about the business of making the ships ready. The sun was getting low, the river was running high, charging by in its endless liquid hurry, sighing and gurgling. Casting one last glance up into Havasu, we cut ourselves loose and abandoned ourselves to the current. It felt good to have the bow oar in my grasp once again. The darkening walls swept past us at incredible speed.

"This is the highest water we've seen yet:" Silas announced from behind the mast. "We're going to be lucky to find a good place to camp. Look! Not an uncovered beach in sight!"

There were no side canyons for quite a ways. Churning our oars to center our craft in the current around bend after bend, we waited for a glimpse of a hospitable shelf or beach. Beyond each corner we were confronted by the endless plunging black granite walls, striking straight down into the river on either side.

A few low beaches appeared from time to time, but no campsite. You never know exactly what those guys are doing with that Glen Canyon dam. The water can rise or drop 6 or 7 feet in a few hours... all for the sake of generating electricity for the folks in the city.

I looked back to the stern. Murdock and Ludwig stood stoutly by their oars; Pearce and Silas clung to the rigging beside the mast. The ladies crouched invisibly among the gear, clinging to the lashings which held it secure...

Murdock had joined our crew. Murdock: his black eyes flashed from the stern. I saw him now as if for the first time. Gone was the jovial small-town Doctor from Kansas. In his place stood a Mediterranean man: an Arab or a Greek. Ludwig stood by his side, intent on peering into the twilight before us, downriver.

"Mountain Sheep!" cried Silas. We all craned our heads as he pointed, red beard wagging with excitement. Halfway up the sheer north wall of the canyon, prancing lightly from ledge to ledge, were three wild mountain sheep... airy, light and silent as spirits. Then they stood stock still to observe us, two floating piles of strange apes, passing below...

I glanced ahead and saw that the current was carrying us too far toward the outside as the next bend! Too close to the wall!

"Move right!" I cried, digging my blade deep into the crests of the river's waves. Scudding along next to the over-hanging wall, we wrestled to pull the boat back out toward midstream, ducking low-hanging blocks of granite which hung from the undercut roof close above our heads! The mast skipped within inches of that jagged ceiling, miraculously avoiding a splintering collision.

We spied a shelf on the opposite side of the river. Small, shaped by the current like a huge sand teardrop nestled against the granite, it climbed fifteen or twenty feet above the level of the river and offered us a place to camp. Surging against our oars, Pearce and Silas manning the rarely-used side oars as well, we made for the beach. We tied up the boats; we unloaded them; we unpacked the food, set fires, drank...

Later, on that same night while sitting alone on a tear-shaped beach, I emerged out of a dream-like reverie for a moment and suddenly realized that the river was dropping rapidly, leaving our craft high and dry on the rocks. We men awakened each other and bent our shoulders to the ropes and gunwales, shoving the hulking assemblages of rubber and wood back into the edge of the water.

We lay down on the sand to sleep but Silas began shaking his head and pounding his fist against his temple, claiming to have something lodged in his ear.

"It's alive!" he said. "The little bugger's clawing away at my eardrum!" he yelped, dancing around in a little circle. "It's so loud! It sounds like he's in the center of my brain!"

Murdock, the doctor, appeared with a flashlight. "I can't see anything, Silas", he exclaimed, peering into Silas's hairy lobe. "Wait! I see something moving! He's backing out!" We all watched in amazement as a brown beetle a full inch in length, emerged, tail first, from Silas's head.

"Jesus Christ No wonder it was driving you crazy!" Murdock bemusedly exclaimed. "I thought you'd just gone batty, 'cause he was so far in there that I couldn't even see him!"

We were getting more and more wound up, tight, a bit nervous, hushed: we were approaching Lava Falls, the biggest rapids in the canyon.

We tied up on a broad alluvial beach below Mohawk canyon at the end of the next day. No one except for old Silas, always ready to take another little exploratory hike, even bothered to move from their campfires that night. You would have thought they were all sitting on death row, nothing but a low murmuring of voices rose, the occasional tinkling of pots and spoons as we forced quantities of food into tight stomachs. Silas eventually returned from the mouth of Mohawk canyon. His announcement that he had seen more mountain sheep and a fox fell on numb ears. Everyone's mind was withdrawn, coiled and recoiled into tight little balls of carefully organized energy.

The next morning we lashed the gear tightly around the masts to the decks of the boats and floated to the brink of Lava Falls, tying into the shore just above the tumbling water. We walked down the shore to survey, plan and settle our routes through the gushing descent.

To me the water was feeling like a playmate, and I would gladly commit myself to its most glorious white foam, abandoning my fate to its inevitable kindness. But again and again I paced the shore with Silas, Pearce, and Ludwig, beginning our evaluation of the lower holes, the boat-eating hearts of the rapids that must be avoided, working our way up the shore again and again, casting sticks into the foam to observe the pathways of the currents, planning every detail of our entry from above, our strokes to this side and that, threading a flawless route in our minds' eyes, one which would bring us into the boiling places low in the rapids across the ridges and bridges of spuming water between the holes. The huge rock on the right projected outwards from the shore, damming up half the channel and creating a giant, pulsing surf! That is what we ought most to avoid...

Meanwhile, Abner, Murdock, Slevin and Scott paced the rocks just as we were, likewise bent on deciphering the route for their boat. A flotilla of commercial boatmen appeared, motors roaring, and put in beside us to survey the same scene. Their passengers scampered out onto shore, delighted at the prospect of watching our motor-less crafts tackle the waves. But we waited, conferred, observed and judged. A couple of motorized craft cast off, throttled in an arch, upstream across the river, a feat inconceivable for our oared craft, and entered the tongue of the rapids from far right side, between the mammoth submerged boulders which guard the top of the rapids, and powered their way to the left for all they were worth, skimming past the giant projecting slab from a safe distance, huge rubber doughnuts of boats rippling and folding over the waves, troughs and holes, too big to be sucked in and spit out like our little rubber ducklings.

Conferring, we agreed that to enter the top of the rapids from so far to the right would be disastrous for us, as we would have no hope of rowing our way across the current and avoid the huge slab below. Two possible routes had revealed themselves to us. One would bring us into the top of the rapids at the center, skimming between another two of those uppermost boulders and then flailing away with oars to the left side in order to miss the big slab. The other, the one which I had begun to prefer, involved slipping between a larger number of rocks in the upper left part of the rapids, gradually working our way to the right until we would arrive in the center of the current, far to the left of and safe from the giant slab, holding all the while to shallower water. Abner preferred the first alternative and set off, huge man, barrel chest and belly, hunkered over his bow oar, Scott and Murdock on the stern. Accurately slipping between the upper gates to the rapids, the bow plunged deep into a hole which had been nearly, invisible from shore, so covered up with froth and foam had it been. The entire boat vanished into that hole, only the tip of the mast with its fluttering orange flag remained visible above all that cascading liquid. At the next moment the nose of the boat reappeared, soaring up out of the river like a giant porpoise, Abner holding onto that bow oar as if it was the reins of a runaway steed, crew and passengers still intact behind, water streaming off their faces and limbs.

We stood on the shore with mouths open wide, cheering frantically over their re-appearance. But then next thing we knew, it looked as if the hand of a giant and slumbering river god, a monstrously barnacled old titan who lay reclining in the rocks beneath the rapids, had casually grasped the bow of Abner's boat, pinching it by the nose and lackadaisically giving it a spin. A few frantic oar strokes to no avail, and there they were, flying stern first in the very center of the current headed directly for the awful whirlpool-generating slab on the right side of the river below. We gaped in horror from the shore as the boat plunged, faster and faster, on top of that disaster-bound ridge of water. Beside the giant slab, the boat swung around, placing bow foremost once again. Then a huge watery backlash from the edge of the whirlpool swept beneath the boat from the side, lifting it up into the air. Tilting vertically on its left edge, it flowed downstream, falling neither upside down nor

back onto its bottom. In slow motion, so it seemed, we watched person after person slide and tumble off into the river; Abner, Scott, Murdock, Nicole... Only Monica and Slevin remained, clinging to the lashing and to the mast...

Gratefully, we watched the boat tumble back down onto the water right-side- up... if only the swimming crew can either clamber back onto the boat or make it to shore, the worst of the rapids is over. We see one swimmer headed for shore: Murdock it later turned out to have been. He had curled himself into a little ball, was sucked deep down into the roiling hole, holding his breath, his glasses clutched pitifully in the grasp of one of his hands, until the whirling currents choked him back out onto the surface and he drew a grateful inhalation and began swimming for shore. Abner had plunged into the water, resurfacing under the boat, as did Nicole. He soon bobbed out beside the bow; Nicole pushed herself this way and that, trapped beneath the boat's bottom for almost too long, trying to find its edge! At last she found it and her head popped out into the air. Monica and Scott surfaced with ease beside the boat and all began clambering back aboard. All we could see was a tangling and twisting of arms and legs, a be-drenched craft with a broken mast limping downstream; who was there and who might not be, we couldn't tell.

The commercial boat passengers must have been gawking from the shore as were we, but we didn't see them, hear them or think about them.

We headed up-shore to our craft, hearts wildly pounding, anxious to follow our friends down to offer any help we could should their struggle persist. One of the commercial boatmen grabbed me by the arm as I raced by.

"Are you going to go the same way?" he asked.

"No," I replied. "We're going to enter the top further to the left."

"Not further toward the left!" he cried. "That's certain disaster! I've seen other boats try that and they can't make it! There are too many rocks on that side of the river and there's a shelf..."

But I was already gone. The route was fixed in my mind. I had looked at it too long, hard and carefully to be able to give credence to his words.

At a run, I pursued the others toward our boat. Half-way there I was confronted by Sandra, pale and shaking, saun-

tering back down the trail. She gave me a fearful look, lowered her eyes to the ground, then raised them again…

"I'm sorry," she trembled. "I can't go. One of the commercial boatmen has agreed to take me down on a boat with motor. He'll drop me off wherever you land…"

"Ok," I said, feeling her peel off like a sparrow from the edge of the flock.

Silas, Pearce, Ludwig, Sonia and Joy were already there, coiling the bow and stern lines, checking their handholds in the rigging. I climbed onto the bow, lashed down the oar so it wouldn't fly off its pin, gave a nod to Ludwig to shove us off… Pulling our way out into the current, we began searching, feeling for the right spot: it's all in being able to enter the top of the

rapids at exactly the right spot! I scanned the river downstream for the protruding boulders which I had selected from shore to be our landmarks. To recognize them from an entirely new angle is not always easy, not always possible, and sometimes the top of the rapids must be entered with uncertainty, a best guess...

But this time I was too well prepared to miss. I spied the recognizable rocks and waves and ripples: there, immediately beneath the left side of the bow, a red rock. That's the one! We were in exactly the right place.

Uh oh! I felt a shallow boulder grab the end of my oar... Going through the rapids with a shattered bow oar or with the oar pushed irrevocably off its pin is to commit yourself to the hands of the river and fate. That had happened to me three years earlier upriver in Hance rapids. This time we were luckier and the boulder let go, the oar slipped free unharmed and still tied onto its pin.

We were halfway down the rapids and the deck wasn't even wet! Zigging and zagging around another couple of boulders, hauling to the right to miss a large hole on our left... we're

home free, riding the crest of the central tongue, far from the grasp of the huge slab on the right. We emerge from the lower rapids, ride a few percussion waves, the kind that are nothing but fun to ride, the dancing water ponies, they kick us around a little bit, a crest or two moisten our feet, and that's it! We're through!

Abner's crew has managed to anchor their battered craft to the right side of the river a quarter of a mile downstream; Murdock has reached shore, replaced his glasses, and run down to rejoin them. They're all ok, all in the midst of giving gasping accounts of what happened to each of them. We pulled in beside them; they scarcely realized that we had arrived; they stood clinging to each other, panting and exclaiming...

"Did you hear what happened to Nicole?" Slevin asked me.

"No."

"She was trapped under the boat for a long time! Every time she tried to swim upward she would bump into it again! She was really passing out by the time she finally found her way out! She really almost drowned! And last spring she had had a dream with the exact same scene... So being trapped under the raft had an eerie deja vue feeling about it... it was a really close call..."

Little Joy came up to me, eyes shining, wrapped her arms around me, gave me a big hug. "We ran it perfectly!" she jubilated.

Ludwig came up to me and shook my hand saying, "Congratulations!"

But Pearce declared, "We should have run it the same way Abner tried! Our way wasn't even exciting: We didn't even get the deck wet!"

The commercial boat brushed ashore above us for just a moment, giving time for Sandra to hop ashore. Then the boatman took his huge rubber doughnut slithering downriver past us, his passengers waving and cheering at us. Sandra approached us meekly, silently. There was a feeling that suddenly she had become an outsider: the one who had abandoned ship. I had felt similarly six years earlier when I had swum for shore after the raft I was on became hung on a rock at the top of a waterfall in the Big Drop in Cataract Canyon. I had seen the danger coming. It wasn't my boat. I wasn't the "captain." But stories were told about me which cast me in an unheroic light. I walked up to Sandra and gave her a squeeze to let her know that she was still one of us.

Murdock couldn't remember if he'd been swept off Abner's boat before everyone else or not. Breathless stories raged

and tumbled on the subject amongst Abner's crew, food-boxes
were dragged out and broken open, a general sort of celebra-
tion began. Through the jaws of disaster and safely out the other side! Some good sized rapids remained below us on the river, but they would seem like the playful buffets of kitten paws
after Lava. For the rest of the afternoon we floated lazily down

the river, toying with whatever rapids remained. We pulled our tired muscles ashore onto another sandy delta. We all stuffed our aching but relieved bones into bedrolls and lost ourselves in immediate slumber.

The next morning a rather sullen crew arose and haphazardly loaded the boats. Today would be our last day on the river. Minds began turning toward the outside world beyond the rim. We set ourselves adrift on a slow and dreary current. Not much drop in that part of the river. Few bothered to don life preservers; few talked. Tired of running the oars we swapped off on the task as frequently as possible. As if to further torment us, the canyon suddenly produced a long series of up-river gusts: a headwind. The broad rubber sides of the boats were behaving like sails and our progress down the slow river sagged to practically nothing. Pearce and I occupied ourselves by manufacturing a couple of parachutes from army ponchos and alpine cord. Deployed into the central current, these "mules" served to fasten us more strongly to the downstream pull of the river. Seeing our success with the gimmicks, Abner's crew soon unleashed one of their own "mules" into the water and some sort of ponderous race began. The "mules" required continuous managing. The slightest side eddy in the current could divert one of the brainless, rudderless contraptions into some monotonously churning side whirlpool where the "mule" could begin straining upstream, raft in tow.

Hugging the bank like nervous rock climbers on a narrow ledge, we approached our take-out point at Diamond Creek. If we missed that landing and spun helplessly downriver, we would be days floating down to another takeout point.

The huge pointed nipple of Diamond Peak marked our destination; we watched it slowly grow more intimate as we closed in on it, rounding bend after bend in the river. The canyon below Diamond Peak faded into some meaningless anonymity: the land beyond the pale, the yarn to be left unspun, the song to be left unsung.... a part of the land through which we were not destined to pass. Somewhere down there lay Lake

Mead, reportedly a vile and stagnant swamp created by the dam. We would not see it. It belonged to another time, another age. We were about to wrest ourselves from the grasp of the canyon.

Hopping ashore for the last time... a dull thump under our feet as we landed on solid ground to stay for some time, some months, a year perhaps... How long before I would find myself on the river once again? ...everyone asked himself silently as his feet struck the sand.

A pickup truck full of Hualapai Indians from Peach Springs were enjoying themselves for the last time by the edge of the river, trying to conjure up enough sobriety to venture back up the road from whence they had come.

Pearce and Slevin and I approached. "Hi!"

"Hi!"

"Are you guys going back to Peach Springs soon? Do you suppose we could have a ride so we can bring our trucks down?" we asked.

"Sure, I figure you can come. We'll, be goin' along pretty soon... soon as we get wet one more time!"

"Get wet! Get wet!" the 5 or 6 young men cried, splashing water over each other's faces. "Moose! Get up! Get wet!" A 300 pound fellow named "Moose" was already asleep in the truck bed. He didn't have it in him to make it down to the river to get wet one more time.

Slevin and Pearce and I wound our way up the road with the Hualapais twenty miles or so to Peach Springs. We stopped from time to time beside the creek so that everyone could pile off and "get wet" one more time. We got to exchange happy smiles with their friends as we rolled into town. We were in the right company and were spared the usual deadpan expressions reserved for white folks.

We made our way toward our trucks, gave our thanks to Moose and his friends and went into a little cafe for hamburgers and coffee. A slick be-sunglassed couple obviously driving back from California to New York came in. How strange to be back out in this world beyond the rim. The coastal culture couple sat in smoky silence, their beings apparently diffuse, invisible.

Out here one can forget... forget whatever it is one is trying to remember... Every minute spent outside the canyon walls seemed to me to be a violation of sacred space... It felt confusing.

"Let's take the trucks back down and begin loading up the rafts," Slevin concluded. So we bounced our way back down to the river, trucks whining, grinding and lurching away in low gears.

As we approached our friends Abner suggested, "I think we ought to keep it down a bit. See those guys over there?" There were four guys unloading a raft just a ways down the shore. "Those guys are rangers from the Park. They gave us a lot of shit when they first pulled up... especially one of them... the other three actually seem like pretty mellow guys..."

"What happened?"

"They came over and told us that they'd received a. lot of complaints about our nudity from the passing commercial crowds. I explained to them that we all know each other and that after we've been down in the canyon for a while we start to get pretty relaxed; that we're not interested in trying to offend anybody... Three of them seemed pretty loose, but that one guy pointed at Scott and said, 'Well, if you're not trying to offend anybody, tell your friend over there to put some pants on!' And he sort of huffed off over to their boat there. I suggest we load up the boats and get on the road. Of course we're outside of the Park here so those rangers don't really have any authority here anyway... But they might make it difficult next time we try and get another permit...!"

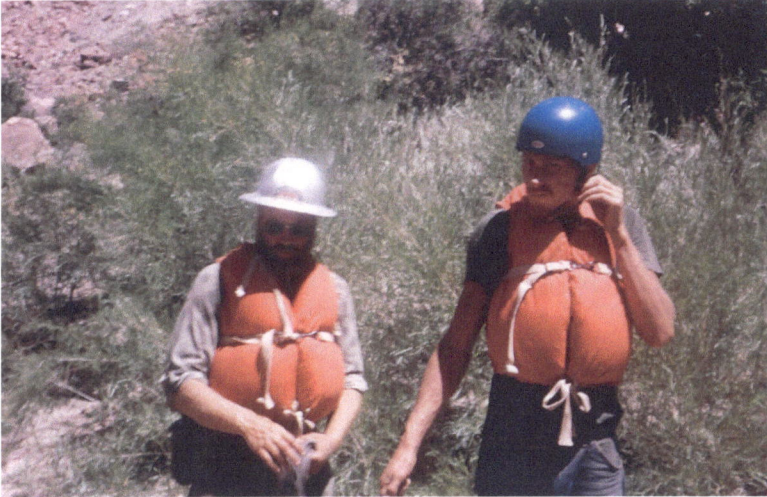

A couple of the Park Rangers returned and hovered around us as we unlaced, unbolted and unscrewed our rigs, chatting amicably with us about raft construction... I assumed that these were the ones that were "pretty loose..." We made a few comments about the lashing, the general sea-worthiness of the crafts... The truth of the matter is that they were drawn to our colorfully flagged pirate vessels and wanted to make an effort to be part of our river-rat gang.

A Ranger truck appeared. They flopped their little doughnut of a rig onto it and disappeared up the road.

Just before dark we finally finished piling the last pieces onto our trucks and we began the slow grind uphill back to Peach Springs, then east toward Grand Canyon Village where a number of our cars had been left parked. Late that night, we pulled off the road and slept near Seligman.

The next morning I awoke feeling the pressure of someone's head sleeping against my knee. I looked down. An old man, an Indian, was huddled against me for warmth. The sun was just appearing over the horizon and I pulled myself gently out of my sleeping bag. I looked around. Pearce, Abner, others were sitting up, rubbing their eyes, trying to take in this new chilly beyond-the-rim world in which we suddenly were finding ourselves. I pointed to the old Indian, who lay, thin and emaciated as a rail, ribs showing through the shirt on his back, on the ground beside me. I wrapped the sleeping bag around him and went about cleaning the spark plugs in the '53 Ford truck. Eventually the old man awoke, picked himself up onto his feet and wobbled over to where we were working on the truck.

"I Na...wo meai...," he announced.

"What?" I asked.

He repeated himself, slurring words beyond recognition, brain cells apparently burnt out by too many years of alcohol, but eventually I realized he was telling us that he was a Navajo mechanic. He pointed at the carburetor and said, "ca... wea..."

"Carburetor!" Pearce agreed.

"Mmm!" the old man agreed, his tone serious and businesslike.

Soon it turned out that the old fellow had been up on his feet again for too long. He began to collapse, go limp, as he continually struggled to peer into the engine compartment of the truck. I wrapped my arms around him.

I lowered him back onto one of our ponchos on the ground. I put my hands on his back. The ribs and vertebrae were sharp beneath the skin, like sticks inside an old tattered leather bag. As soon as I touched him over the backbone he began moaning semi-consciously with deep relief. I could feel the nearly extinct nerve inside his spine drawing on the life energy in my hands, sucking the electricity like a hungry run-down battery. It didn't matter whether I gently rubbed the bones or just left my hands lying in that spot, the old fellow groaned and moaned with primordial pleasure. I had no idea how much life was actually flowing apparently out of my hands and into his central nervous system, but it seemed like it might serve the poor fellow for a few more days perhaps... a number of hours at least. It began to lightly rain. We covered the old fellow. He looked like a skeleton anxious for the cleansing, sun-bleaching process to begin, but deep behind those sunken eyes the life force flickered, jovial as ever... essentially the same as always... just sunken, withdrawn, recessed into the core of the man. Sandra wandered over to my side as I continued pressing gently over those essential central vertebrae. She had caught a little brown lizard. Gently, with care, she placed the lizard on the man's cheek. Leaving the poncho behind, we climbed into the trucks and resumed our journey towards Grand Canyon Village.

Not everyone could fit into or onto the trucks so Pearce and I stood beside the highway with our thumbs out. Finally, after an hour or so, a vehicle was approaching. Just as it drew near and we were imagining how the driver must be checking us out, weighing the pros and cons of picking us up, I felt a fiery pain on my balls. In a dancing frenzy I undid my pants and found the culprit: a nasty red ant. So much for that potential ride!

But sooner or later a driver took pity on us and thus began a series of rides which, after a day or so, delivered us back to Steamboat Springs where we said our goodbyes for now to others who had ridden back on the trucks.

And we all began the dis-orienting task of re-integrating back into this strange world we call civilization.

To enjoy a 6-minute video from one of our Grand Canyon river trips in 1971, go to:
https://vimeo.com/album/2898421/video/147192873

# Other Books by Cameron Powers

**Singing in Baghdad:**
A Musical Mission of Peace

**Spiritual Traveler:**
Journeys Beyond Fear

**Arabic Musical Scales with 2 Audio CDs:**
Basic Maqam Teachings

**Harmonic Secrets of Arabic Music Scales With 2 Audio CDs:**
Fine Tuning the Maqams

The books listed above can be ordered from:
www.gldesignpub.com
or write for more info:
E-Mail: distrib@gldesignpub.com

www.ingramcontent.com/pod-product-compliance
Lightning Source LLC
Chambersburg PA
CBHW041228270326
41935CB00002B/8

9 781933 983202